WILLIAM WALTON

THE TWELVE

An Anthem for the Feast of any Apostle

for SATB soli, mixed chorus, and organ
(or orchestra)

Words by W. H. AUDEN

ORCHESTRATION

Double woodwind	Tuba
4 Horns	Timpani
2 Trumpets	Percussion
3 Trombones	Harp
Strings	

Duration: 11 minutes

Full scores and orchestral parts are on hire

This work was given its first performance (with organ)
on 16 May 1965 by the choir of Christ Church, Oxford,
directed by Sydney Watson.

MUSIC DEPARTMENT

OXFORD
UNIVERSITY PRESS

The Twelve

I

Without arms or charm of culture,
Persons of no importance
From an unimportant Province,
They did as the Spirit bid,
Went forth into a joyless world
Of swords and rhetoric
To bring it joy.

When they heard the Word, some demurred, some mocked, some were
shocked: but many were stirred and the Word spread. Lives long dead were
quickened to life; the sick were healed by the Truth revealed; released into
peace from the gin of old sin, men forgot themselves in the glory of the story
told by the Twelve.
Then the Dark Lord, adored by this world, perceived the threat of the Light to
his might. From his throne he spoke to his own. The loud crowd, the sedate
engines of State, were moved by his will to kill. It was done. One by one, they
were caught, tortured, and slain.

II

O Lord, my God,
Though I forsake thee
Forsake me not,
But guide me as I walk
Through the valley of mistrust,
And let the cry of my disbelieving absence
Come unto thee,
Thou who declared unto Moses:
"I shall be there."

III

Children play about the ancestral graves, for the dead no longer walk.
Excellent still in their splendour are the antique statues: but can do neither
   good nor evil.
Beautiful still are the starry heavens: but our fate is not written there.
Holy still is speech, but there is no sacred tongue: the Truth may be told in all.
Twelve as the winds and the months are those who taught us these things:
   envisaging each in an oval glory, let us praise them all with a merry noise.

The Twelve

W. H. Auden
(1907–1973)

WILLIAM WALTON

Taken from *Shorter Choral Works without Orchestra*, William Walton Edition, vol. 6, edited by Timothy Brown (Oxford, 1999), where full critical apparatus may be found.

forth into a joyless world Of swords and rhetoric To bring

SOPRANO I
Joy, joy,

SOPRANO II

ALTO I
To bring it joy, joy,

ALTO II

TENOR I
To bring it joy, joy,

TENOR II
To bring it joy, joy, joy,

BASS I * (SOLO)
it joy, to bring it joy, joy,

BASS II
it joy, to bring it joy, joy, joy,

* When the opening is sung by Bass Solo, Tutti Basses I & II enter at [

men for - got them-selves ... in the glo - (o) -

sin,____ ... men for - got them-selves in the glo - (o) -

cresc.

Ped.

CHOIRS I & II

- (o) -ry ... of the sto - (o) - (o) -ry, ... in the glo - ry of__ the

* Or solo treble, or a few voices.

* Or solo treble, or a few voices.

* If available, a male alto.   † Or a few voices.

* Preferably boys if available.   † Or a few voices.

22

27

Printed in England by Caligraving Ltd, Thetford, Norfolk